FLYING INSECTS

By Patricia Lantier-Sampon
Illustrated by Timothy Spransy

Gareth Stevens Publishing
MILWAUKEE

For a free color catalog describing Gareth Stevens' list of high-quality books, call 1-800-341-3569 (USA) or 1-800-461-9120 (Canada).

Library of Congress Cataloging-in-Publication Data

Lantier-Sampon, Patricia.
    Flying insects / by Patricia Lantier-Sampon; illustrations
by Timothy Spransy.
       p. cm. — (Wings)
    Includes index.
    ISBN 0-8368-0542-9
    1. Insects—Juvenile literature. 2. Insects—Flight—Juvenile
literature. [1. Insects. 2. Flight.] I. Spransy, Timothy, ill. II. Title. III.
Series: Lantier-Sampon, Patricia — Wings.
QL467.2.L36 1994
595.7—dc20
                              91-50347

Edited, designed, and produced by
Gareth Stevens Publishing
1555 North RiverCenter Drive, Suite 201
Milwaukee, Wisconsin 53212, USA

Designer: Kristi Ludwig

Printed in the United States of America

1 2 3 4 5 6 7 8 99 98 97 96 95 94

Contents

Insects have helped us learn how to fly; they've given us lessons and now share the sky!

Crickets

Crickets can jump and hurdle and spring. And some have a marvelous talent — they sing!

Butterflies

Butterflies flit and flutter and dance. They sip flower nectar at every chance.

Beetles

Beetles can crawl and wriggle and creep. Some wave their antennae in the dark while we sleep!

8

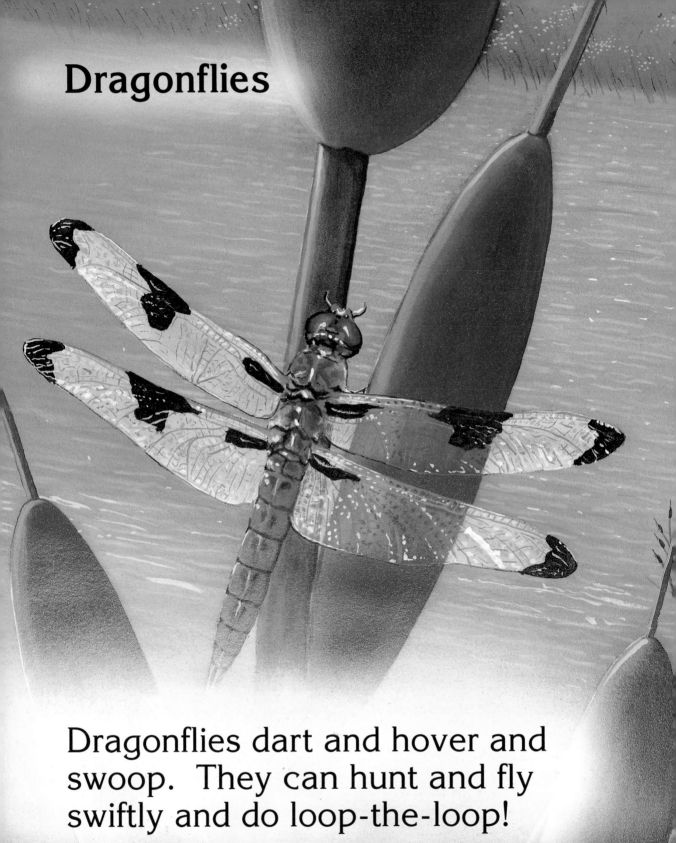

Dragonflies

Dragonflies dart and hover and swoop. They can hunt and fly swiftly and do loop-the-loop!

Grasshoppers

Grasshoppers jump and skitter and swarm. Sometimes they eat healthy crops on the farm.

Honeybees

Honeybees buzz and bumble and drone. They work to make honey as soon as they're grown.

Wasps

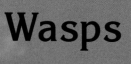

Wasps whisper and hum as they waltz on the wing. And, oh, the attention their stingers can bring!

16

Fireflies

Fireflies flash and flicker and glimmer. They search for their mates with a luminous shimmer.

18

Mosquitoes

Mosquitoes are pesty and pesky
and smart. They zoom in on
dinner with a quick, stinging dart!

Houseflies

Houseflies are tiny and crafty and greedy. They'll eat anything tasty, and they're awfully speedy!

22

Flying is fun for both people
and insects. Isn't it grand to
have wings?

Glossary

antennae: movable organs on the heads of insects that are used mainly for touching and smelling.

hover: to stay in the same place or to hang with a fluttering motion in the air.

hurdle: to hop or leap over something.

luminous: making or giving off a shining light.

nectar: a sweet juice that is found in some plants.

Index